✍ **W9-BUI-495**

The Playtime
treasury.

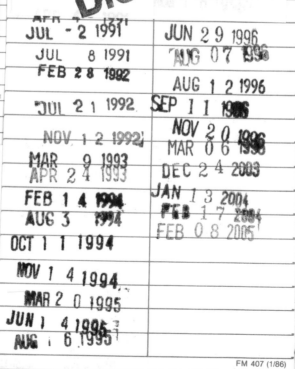

DATE DUE

APR 1991	
JUL - 2 1991	JUN 2 9 1996
JUL 8 1991	AUG 0 7 1996
FEB 2 8 1992	AUG 1 2 1996
JUL 2 1 1992	SEP 1 1 1996
NOV 1 2 1992	NOV 2 0 1996
MAR 9 1993	MAR 0 6 1998
APR 2 4 1993	DEC 2 4 2003
FEB 1 4 1994	JAN 1 3 2004
AUG 3 1994	FEB 1 7 2004
OCT 1 1 1994	FEB 0 8 2005
NOV 1 4 1994	
MAR 2 0 1995	
JUN 1 4 1995	
AUG 1 6 1995	

FM 407 (1/86)

THE
playtime
TREASURY

For Poppy and Daisy

THE
playtime
TREASURY

*A collection of playground rhymes,
games, and action songs*

Selected by
PIE CORBETT

Illustrated by
MOIRA AND COLIN MACLEAN

DOUBLEDAY
NEW YORK LONDON TORONTO SYDNEY AUCKLAND

Published by Doubleday
a division of Bantam Doubleday Dell Publishing Group, Inc.
666 Fifth Avenue, New York, New York 10103

Doubleday
and the portrayal of an anchor with a dolphin
are trademarks of Doubleday,
a division of Bantam Doubleday Dell Publishing Group, Inc.

Library of Congress Cataloging-in-Publication Data
The Playtime treasury/selected by Pie Corbett; illustrated by Moira
and Colin Maclean. — 1st ed.
p.   cm.
Summary: An illustrated collection of games, rhymes, and songs
involving guessing, choosing, pretending, counting, clapping, and
acting.
1. Games—Juvenile literature.   2. Singing games—Juvenile
literature.   [1. Games.]   I. Corbett, Pie.   II. Maclean, Moira,
ill.   III. Maclean, Colin, 1930–   ill.
GV1203.P58   1990
793—dc20   89-17177   CIP   AC

ISBN 0-385-26448-8

This selection copyright © 1989 by Pie Corbett
Illustrations copyright © 1989 by Colin and Moira Maclean

ALL RIGHTS RESERVED
PRINTED IN PORTUGAL
FIRST EDITION IN THE UNITED STATES OF AMERICA, 1990
0690

 # PREFACE

This anthology steals onto children's own territory, for these are the rhymes and games of the street, the backyard, the playground, and the village. The poetry of playtime links us with our past and reaches out across all nations. You may know these games by different names or with different rules. The game called "Chase," for example, has over thirty different names in Britain alone and is known as "The Lion" in China and "Touch Tag" in New York. Up to the last moment our youngest advisers were telling us, "Oh no, we don't play it like that anymore."

I have tried to present and preserve part of children's culture. Too many children no longer have the opportunity to play together. They live in places where there are no suitable play areas or go to schools that do not allow skipping ropes in the playground. I hope that this book gets tattered and torn in the discovery of playtime. Through their games, children begin to learn how to lose, how to play fair, how to cooperate, how to win with grace, and how to enjoy the thrill of the game itself. They learn the importance of playing within established rules. In many ways they are finding out how to relate to each other — possibly the most important skill we ever need to learn.

I have had a lot of fun collecting these rhymes and games. I saw intricate dances and heard repetitive songs which reminded me that where the traditions of play and poetry are woven into one they bind us together as a world tribe. The echo of distant voices stirred memories of my own childhood — I hope that you, too, can rediscover with your children something of that time. For the mystery of poetry and the significance of the game are sheer magic. Any child knows that.

CONTENTS

ACTION RHYMES AND SINGING GAMES 13

A selection of follow the leader games, fingerplays,
counting songs, story rhymes to sing and mime,
and scary rhymes.

DANCING RINGS AND GAMES 31

Traditional and modern singing games
danced in a circle.

HAND-CLAPPING RHYMES 49

Familiar songs to clap to, from delightful rhythmic
chants to speedy circular hand-clapping games.

I can do the can-can just like this.
I can do the hoola hoop,
I can do the twist,
Queens go curtsy,
Kings go bow,
Boys go, "Hi there!"
Girls go, "Wow!"

ACTION RHYMES
AND
SINGING GAMES

Follow the Leader

☆*One person is chosen to be the leader and everyone follows copying him.*

We are off to Timbuctoo
Would you like to go there, too?
All the way and back again,
You must follow our leader then,
You must follow our leader,
You must follow our leader,
All the way and back again,
You must follow our leader.

Follow my Bangalory Man;
Follow my Bangalory Man;
I'll do all that I ever can
To follow my Bangalory Man.
We'll borrow a horse, and steal a gig,
And round the world we'll do a jig,
And I'll do all that I ever can
To follow my Bangalory Man.

Polly Perkin, hold on to my jerkin
Hold on to my gown,
That's the way we march to town.

Did you ever see a lassie,
A lassie, a lassie,
Did you ever see a lassie
Who acted like this?
This way and that way,
This way and that way,
Did you ever see a lassie
Who acted like this?

☆ *Mime the actions of the leader.*
Change to laddie if a boy is the leader.

When I was a baby,
A baby, a baby,
When I was a baby
How happy I was.

Chorus
I was this way, and that way,
That way, and this way,
When I was a baby
Then this way went I.

Verses
When I was a lady,
A lady, a lady,
When I was a lady,
How happy I was.

When I was a sailor,
A sailor, a sailor,
When I was a sailor,
How happy I was.

☆ *Walk or skip while singing the first verse; stop for the*
chorus and mime the verse. Repeat for each verse.

15

Simple Simon met a pieman,
Going to the fair;
Says Simple Simon to the pieman,
Let me taste your ware.

Says the pieman to Simple Simon,
Show me first your penny;
Says Simple Simon to the pieman,
Indeed I have not any.

SIMON SAYS

Pick one player to be SIMON.
Simon then gives orders to the
other players such as, "Simon
says put your hands in the air."
The other players must obey
immediately but only if they hear
the words "Simon says."

If Simon gives an order without
saying "Simon says" (for
example, "Arms out"), any player
who obeys the order is out.

If Simon gives an order but does
something different (for example,
if she says, "Simon says put your
hands on your hips" but puts her
hands over her eyes), the players
who follow the instruction and
not Simon are out.
The winner is the one who stays
longest in the game. He or she
becomes the next Simon.

This old man, he played one,
He played nick-nack on my drum.
Chorus
Nick-nack, paddy-whack,
Give a dog a bone
This old man came rolling home.

☆ *Mime an appropriate action for each
verse. Repeat chorus after each verse.*

Verses
This old man, he played two,
He played nick-nack on my shoe.

This old man, he played three,
He played nick-nack on my knee.

This old man, he played four,
He played nick-nack on my door.

This old man, he played five,
He played nick-nack on my hide.

This old man, he played six,
He played nick-nack on some sticks.

This old man, he played seven,
He played nick-nack up to heaven.

This old man, he played eight,
He played nick-nack at my gate.

This old man, he played nine,
He played nick-nack on my spine.

This old man, he played ten,
He played nick-nack once again.

Fingerplays

Here is the church,
And here is the steeple,
Open the doors,
And here are the people.

Here is the parson
Going upstairs,
And here is the parson
Saying his prayers.

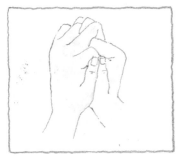

☆ Interlock fingers.

☆ Raise index fingers.

☆ Open thumbs and wriggle fingers.

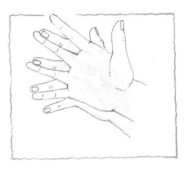

☆ Undo hands. Cross wrists and interlace fingers back to back.

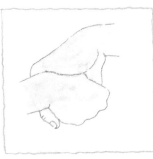

☆ Rotate wrists until palms face each other, fingers curled inside.

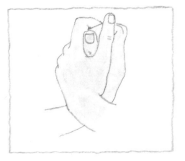

☆ Wriggle thumb.

Snail, snail, put out your horns,
And I'll give you bread and barley corns.

☆ Make a fist, tucking your thumb inside. Lift little finger and index finger to make horns.

Incey wincey spider
Climbing up the spout,
Down came the rain
And washed the spider out.

Out came the sunshine,
Dried up all the rain,
Incey wincey spider
Climbing up again.

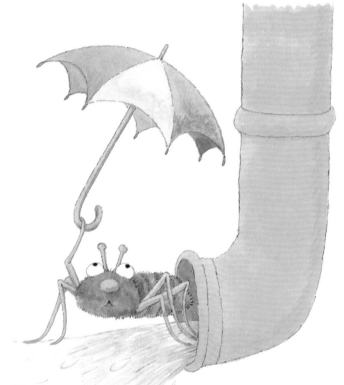

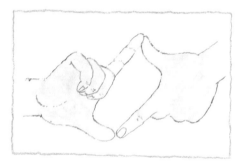

☆ *Climb up by touching opposite
thumb and index fingers.*

Counting songs

Peter works with one hammer,
One hammer, one hammer;
Peter works with one hammer,
All day long.

Verses
Peter works with two hammers . . .
Peter works with three hammers . . .
Peter works with four hammers . . .
Peter works with five hammers . . .

☆ *Hammer in time to the verse using one fist,
then two, then two fists and one foot, then
two fists and both feet. At FIVE, fists, feet, and
head nod to the beat*

One little elephant went out one day,
Upon a spider's web to play;
He had such tremendous fun,
He sent for another elephant to come.

Two little elephants went out one day,
Upon a spider's web to play;
They had such tremendous fun,
They sent for another elephant to come.

Three little elephants went out one day,
Upon a spider's web to play;
They had such tremendous fun,
They sent for another elephant to come . . .

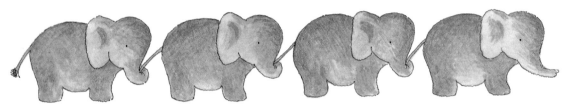

☆ *Choose someone to be the first elephant. He walks around swinging one arm like an elephant's trunk. At the end of the verse the first elephant chooses a second elephant, who holds on to him with her "trunk." Continue until everyone is an elephant!*

Un éléphant se balançait,
Sur une toile d'araignée,
Il trouva ça si amusant,
Qu'il appèla un autre éléphant.

☆ *The French version.*

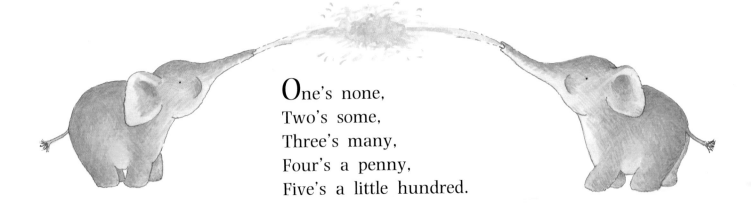

One's none,
Two's some,
Three's many,
Four's a penny,
Five's a little hundred.

Five little speckled frogs
Sat on a speckled log
Eating the most delicious bugs —
Yum, yum.
One jumped into the pool
Where it was nice and cool,
Then there were four more speckled frogs.
Glub, glub!

☆ Squat on the floor like frogs. One by one take it in turns to be the frog that jumps into the pool. Repeat the song each time, counting down. Teddy bears and other toys make good frogs if you haven't enough players.

Verses
Four little speckled frogs . . .
Three little speckled frogs . . .
Two little speckled frogs . . .

One little speckled frog
Sat on a speckled log
Eating the most delicious bugs —
Yum, yum.
He jumped into the pool
Where it was nice and cool,
Now there are no more speckled frogs.
Glub, glub!

Story rhymes

There was a princess long ago,
Long ago, long ago,
There was a princess long ago,
Long, long ago.

☆ *Begin by choosing a* PRINCESS, *a* WICKED
FAIRY, *and a* PRINCE. *The princess stands in
the center of a ring. The singing should be
slow until you reach the last verse.*

And she lived in a big high tower,
A big high tower, a big high tower,
And she lived in a big high tower,
Long, long ago.

☆ *The players raise their hands to make a
tower.*

A wicked fairy waved her wand,
Waved her wand, waved her wand,
A wicked fairy waved her wand,
Long, long ago.

☆ *The wicked fairy waves an imaginary wand
over the princess.*

The princess slept for a hundred
    years,
A hundred years, a hundred years,
The princess slept for a hundred
    years,
Long, long ago.

A great big forest grew around,
Grew around, grew around,
A great big forest grew around,
Long, long ago.

☆ *Everyone waves their arms like trees in the wind.*

A gallant prince came riding by,
Riding by, riding by,
A gallant prince came riding by,
Long, long ago.

☆ *The prince rides around the outside of the circle.*

He chopped the trees down one by one,
One by one, one by one,
He chopped the trees down one by one,
Long, long ago.

☆ *He pretends to chop his way through the circle.*

He took the princess by the hand,
By the hand, by the hand,
He took the princess by the hand,
Long, long ago.

☆ *He takes the princess's hand and she wakes up.*

So everybody's happy now,
Happy now, happy now,
So everybody's happy now,
Happy now.

☆ *The circle skips around faster and faster.*

I have a dog and his name is Rags,
He eats so much that his tummy sags,
His ears flip-flop,
And his tail wig-wags,
And when he walks he goes zig-zag.

Chorus
He goes flip-flop, wig-wag, zig-zag,
He goes flip-flop, wig-wag, zig-zag,
He goes flip-flop, wig-wag, zig-zag,
I love Rags and he loves me.
I love Rags and he loves me.

My dog Rags he loves to play
He rolls around in the mud all day,
I whistle but he won't obey,
He always runs the other way.

☆ *Follow the actions using hands and fingers to imitate the words. Hands at either side of head drop forward for* FLIP-FLOP; *hips wiggle for* WIG-WAG; *arms cross for* ZIG-ZAG; *hands rotate for* ROLLS AROUND; *fingers wiggle for* RUNS THE OTHER WAY, *and so on.*

Little Rabbit Foo Foo
Hopping through the green grass,
Scooping up the field mice,
Knocking them on the head.

☆ *Everyone sits in a circle and two players
are chosen to be* RABBIT FOO FOO *and the*
GOOD FAIRY. *Rabbit Foo Foo hops inside the
circle, pretending to scoop up mice. Then the
good fairy arrives and gives her a number
of chances.*

Down came the good fairy
And she said:
Little Rabbit Foo Foo,
I don't want to see you,
Scooping up the field mice,
Knocking them on the head,
So I'll give you *three* more chances.

☆ *The first verse is repeated with the good
fairy appearing each time to count the
number of chances left. When these are used
up, the good fairy decides what to turn Rabbit
Foo Foo into — a monster, a frog...?*

Little Rabbit Foo Foo
I really warned you;
Now I'm going to turn you
Into a *red-eyed monster*.

25

☆ *Choose two players to be* ROGER *and the* OLD LADY.

Old Roger is dead and he lies in his grave,
Lies in his grave, lies in his grave.
Old Roger is dead and he lies in his grave,
Heigh ho, lies in his grave.

They planted an apple tree over his head,
Over his head, over his head.
They planted an apple tree over his head,
Heigh ho, over his head.

The apples grew ripe and they all tumbled down,
All tumbled down, all tumbled down.
The apples grew ripe and they all tumbled down,
Heigh ho, they all tumbled down.

There came an old woman a-picking them up,
A-picking them up, a-picking them up.
There came an old woman a-picking them up,
Heigh ho, a-picking them up.

Old Roger got up and he gave her a knock,
Gave her a knock, gave her a knock.
Old Roger got up and he gave her a knock,
Heigh ho, gave her a knock.

This made the old woman go hipperty-hop,
Hipperty-hop, hipperty-hop,
This made the old woman go hipperty-hop,
Heigh ho, hipperty-hop,

AIKEN DRUM

There was a man lived in the moon,
   lived in the moon, lived in the moon,
There was a man lived in the moon,
And his name was Aiken Drum.
And he played upon a ladle, a ladle, a ladle,
He played upon a ladle, and his name
   was Aiken Drum.

☆ *Try singing this one while beating household
"instruments" such as spoons and saucepan lids.
Repeat the second verse changing the name of
the instrument each time. The traditional
verses describe Aiken Drum's clothes. Here are
some of them:*

And his hat was made of good cream cheese,
   good cream cheese, good cream cheese,
And his hat was made of good cream cheese,
And his name was Aiken Drum.

And his coat was made of good roast beef,
   good roast beef, good roast beef,
And his coat was made of good roast beef,
And his name was Aiken Drum.

And his buttons were made of penny loaves,
   penny loaves, penny loaves,
And his buttons were made of penny loaves,
And his name was Aiken Drum.

Scary rhymes

Late on a dark and stormy night,
Three witches stirred with all their might.
Two little ghosts said, "How d'ye do?"
The wizard went tiptoe, tiptoe,
Boooooo!

Poor Willy the Witch
Not too rich,
Had a big itch,
Fell in a ditch,
Poor Willy the Witch.

Hinx, minx, the old witch winks,
The fat begins to fry.
Nobody's home but Jumping Joan,
Father, mother, and I.
Stick, stock, stone dead,
Blind men can't see;
Every knave will have a slave,
You and I must be he.

On a dark, dark night,
In a dark, dark wood,
In a dark, dark house,
In a dark, dark room,
In a dark, dark cupboard,
On a dark, dark shelf,
In a dark, dark box,
There was a GHOST.

Three little ghostesses,
Sitting on postesses,
Eating buttered toastesses,
Greasing their fistesses,
Up to their wristesses.
Oh what beastesses,
To make such feastesses.

I said my pajamas,
I slipped on my prayers.
I went up my slippers,
I took off my stairs.
I turned off the bed,
I jumped in the light.
The reason for this is
You gave me a fright!

Bat, bat, come under my hat,
    For here's a slice of bacon,
When I bake, I'll give you cake
    If I am not mistaken.

Here we go dancing jingo-ring,
Jingo-ring, jingo-ring,
Here we go dancing jingo-ring,
About the merry-ma-tanzie.

Twice about and then we fall,
Then we fall, then we fall,
Twice about and then we fall,
About the merry-ma-tanzie.

DANCING RINGS
AND GAMES

Do you know the Muffin Man,
The Muffin Man, the Muffin Man,
Do you know the Muffin Man
Who lives in Drury Lane?

Yes, I know the Muffin Man,
The Muffin Man, the Muffin Man,
Yes, I know the Muffin Man
Who lives in Drury Lane.

Two of us know the Muffin Man,
The Muffin Man, the Muffin Man,
Two of us know the Muffin Man
Who lives in Drury Lane.

☆ *Choose one player to stand in the middle of a ring. The ring dances around to the first verse, then the player in the center picks someone who sings the second verse. These two join hands and dance in the middle singing the third verse.*

Repeat the verses, changing the number of players until everyone is dancing around singing, "We all know the Muffin Man." The game is for six or more players.

Wallflowers, wallflowers, growing up so high.
We're pretty mermaids and we shall not die.
Except for *Sunita*, she's the only one.
Turn her round, turn her round,
So she cannot face the sun.

☆ *Choose one person to be the caller.*
Everyone joins hands in a ring and dances around singing. The caller names someone at EXCEPT FOR *and he or she has to turn around and face outward. Repeat until everyone has turned around and the whole ring is facing outward. This ring game is for five or more players.*

Let's go to Kentucky
Let's go to the fair,
To see a señorita,
With flowers in her hair.
Shake it, shake it, shake it,
Shake it if you can;
Oh, rumble to the bottom,
Rumble to the top,
Round and round,
Round and round,
Until you cannot stop.

☆ *At least five players are needed. Choose one to be the* SEÑORITA. *Everyone else dances around her, stopping on* SHAKE. *The señorita then has to* SHAKE IT *in the middle; on* RUMBLE, *everyone shakes. At the end the señorita spins around and around with her eyes closed and one arm pointing. Whoever she is pointing at when she stops is the next señorita.*

☆ *An odd number of players are needed for this game. Choose one player to stand in the ring; the others choose partners. On the first verse the player in the middle picks another and they dance together around the outside of the ring. Then they join the circle.*

Lou, lou, skip to me lou,
Lou, lou, skip to me lou.
Lou, lou, skip to me lou,
  Skip to me lou, my darling.

Lost my partner, what shall I do?
Lost my partner, what shall I do?
Lost my partner, what shall I do?
  Skip to me lou, my darling.

☆ *Now the player who had her partner stolen skips around the outside of the ring.*

I've found anuvver one, just like you,
I've found anuvver one, just like you,
I've found anuvver one, just like you,
  Skip to me lou, my darling.

☆ *She then chooses someone else's partner to dance around with before standing back in the ring. Then the game and the song start again.*

34

In and out the dusty bluebells,
In and out the dusty bluebells,
In and out the dusty bluebells,
 Who shall be my partner?

Tippitty tappitty on your shoulder,
Tippitty tappitty on your shoulder,
Tippitty tappitty on your shoulder,
 You shall be my partner.

☆ *This is a ring dance for at least six dancers. Everyone stands in a circle holding their hands up high to make an arch between each dancer. One dancer is chosen to start the dance, and as the dancers sing the first verse, she weaves in and out of the arches. On* WHO SHALL BE MY PARTNER *she stops and taps whoever is closest on the shoulder for the second verse. This dancer joins onto the first dancer and they weave in and out again as the first verse is repeated.*

Little Sally Waters, sitting in a saucer,
　Rise, Sally, rise and dry your eyes.
Fly to the east, fly to the west,
　Fly to the one you love the best.

Now you are married, you must be good,
　And help your wife to chop the wood.
You chop it thin and bring it in,
　There's your love with a wedding ring.

☆ *Stand in a circle and choose someone to go in the middle. She sits down until* BEST, *when she gets up and chooses someone from the circle. They both join hands and skip around the ring together for the second verse. The one who was chosen then goes into the middle. Play with at least four people.*

Down in the valley
　Where the green grass grows,
There stands *Charlotte*
　Washing out her clothes,
She sang and she sang
　And she sang so sweet,
She sang for her playmate
　Across the street.

Playmate, playmate,
　Will you come to tea?
Come next Saturday
　At half past three.
Tea cakes, pancakes,
　All for you and me.
Won't we have a lovely time
　At half past three.

☆ *Stand in a circle and choose one dancer to be in the middle. Everyone sings the first verse putting the name of the dancer in the middle into line three. The dancer in the middle chooses a friend from the circle in the second verse and they pretend to have tea. At least four players are needed.*

☆ *A ring dance for five or more players.*

The wind blows low, the wind blows high,
The rain comes scattering down the sky.
She is handsome, she is pretty,
She is the girl of the golden city.
So, *Claire West*, will you marry me?

If you love him, clap your hands,
If you hate him, stamp your feet.

The wind blows low, the wind blows high,
The stars are dropping from the sky,
Claire West thinks she'll die,
For want of the golden city.

Now *Tom Saunders* takes her by the hand,
Now he leads her to the water,
Gives her kisses one-two-three,
Mrs. *West's* handsome daughter.

☆ *Stand in a ring and choose one dancer to stand in the middle. Her name goes into the last line of the first verse. Decide who she will marry and whisper it around. At the end of the second verse she can clap her hands or stamp her feet. At the start of the third verse put in the name of the dancer she will marry. They dance around together.*

Oats and beans and barley grow,
    Oats and beans and barley grow,
But not you nor I nor anyone know,
    How oats and beans and barley grow.

First the farmer sows his seed,
    Then he stands and takes his ease,
Stamps his feet and claps his hands
    And turns around to view the land.

A-waiting for a partner,
    A-waiting for a partner,
Now open the ring and let one in,
    So oats and beans and barley grow.

☆ *Choose someone to be the* FARMER *in the middle of the ring. Everyone dances around for the first verse. Then the Farmer pretends to* SOW *the seed,* STANDS *with his hands on his hips,* STAMPS *his feet,* CLAPS, *and* TURNS *around to look at his land. During the last verse he picks a partner who becomes the next farmer.*

The farmer's in his den,
The farmer's in his den,
E . . . I . . . E . . . I . . . ,
The farmer's in his den.

Verses

The farmer wants a wife . . .

The wife wants a child . . .

The child wants a nurse . . .

The nurse wants a dog . . .

The dog wants a bone . . .

We all pat the bone . . .

☆ *Choose someone to be the* FARMER, *who stands in the middle of a circle. The circle holds hands and moves around clockwise while they sing. The farmer chooses a* WIFE *and she joins him in the middle. She then chooses a* CHILD *and so on until the* DOG *picks someone to be the* BONE. *If you have lots of players — at least fourteen — the ones in the middle form a new circle that moves around in the opposite direction to the outside circle. During the last verse everyone comes into the middle to pat the poor bone. The only good thing about being the bone is that you can be the next farmer.*

Rosy apple, mellow pear,
　　Bunch of roses she shall wear;
Sword and pistol by her side;
　　I know who shall be my bride.

Take her by the lily-white hand,
　　Lead her across the water,
Blow her a kiss and say goodbye,
　　For she's the captain's daughter.

☆ *Stand in a circle holding hands and choose one dancer to stand in the middle. Everyone dances around singing the first verse. Then the dancer in the middle picks the* BRIDE. *These two then form an arch by holding both hands up high. The circle dancers skip under the arch for the second verse. On the last line the arch comes down capturing someone — he or she has to stand in the middle for the next game. At least five players are needed — the more, the better.*

In and out the windows,
In and out the windows,
In and out the windows,
As we have done before.

Stand and face your partner,
Stand and face your partner,
Stand and face your partner,
As we have done before.

Now follow her to London,
Now follow her to London,
Now follow her to London,
As we have done before.

Bow before you leave her,
Bow before you leave her,
Bow before you leave her,
As we have done before.

☆ *This dance requires at least six dancers, who all stand in a
circle holding their hands up high to form arches between
each other. Choose one dancer to skip in and out of the arches
during the first verse. On* STAND AND FACE *he stops by one of
the other dancers and waits. During the third verse he
follows her in and out of the arches. For the last verse they
move to the middle of the ring and bow or curtsy to each
other. The partner becomes the next one in the middle and
the game is repeated until everyone has had a turn.*

☆ Everyone stands in a circle with one dancer in the middle.

There's a brown girl in the ring,
Tra la la la la,
There's a brown girl in the ring,
Tra la la la la,
There's a brown girl in the ring,
Tra la la la la,
For she like sugar and I like plum.

Then you skip across the ocean,
Tra la la la la,
Then you skip across the ocean,
Tra la la la la,
Then you skip across the ocean,
Tra la la la la,
For she like sugar and I like plum.

☆ The dancer skips across the circle.

☆ The dancer wiggles for the MOTION.

Then you show me your motion,
Tra la la la la,
Then you show me your motion,
Tra la la la la,
Then you show me your motion,
Tra la la la la,
For she like sugar and I like plum.

Then you wheel and take your partner,
Tra la la la la,
Then you wheel and take your partner,
Tra la la la la,
Then you wheel and take your partner,
Tra la la la la,
For she like sugar and I like plum.

☆ The dancer chooses a partner and they wheel around.

42

Moonshine tonight, come mek me dance and sing,
Moonshine tonight, come mek me dance and sing;
Me deh rock so, you deh rock so,
Under banyan tree.
Me deh rock so, you deh rock so,
Under banyan tree.

Ladies may curtsy, and gentlemen may bow,
Ladies may curtsy, and gentlemen may bow;
Me deh rock so, you deh rock so,
Under banyan tree.
Me deh rock so, you deh rock so,
Under banyan tree.

Then we join hands, and dance around and around,
Then we join hands, and dance around and around;
Me deh rock so, you deh rock so,
Under banyan tree.
Me deh rock so, you deh rock so,
Under banyan tree.

☆ *Everyone joins hands and dances in a circle to the first verse,*
stands and carries out the action of the second verse, then
joins hands and dances around for the last verse.

THE HOKEY POKEY

You put your right arm in,
Your right arm out,
Your right arm in,
And you shake it all about.
You do the Hokey Pokey,
And you turn around,
That's what it's all about.

Chorus
Oh, the Hokey, Pokey, Pokey!
Oh, the Hokey, Pokey, Pokey!
Oh, the Hokey, Pokey, Pokey!
Knees bend,
Arms stretch,
Ra! Ra! Ra!

☆ *Any number can play but the song is more fun the more dancers there are. Everyone stands in a circle and follows the actions as they sing the verses. For the chorus everyone joins hands and dances into the middle and out three times, bends knees, stretches out arms, and shouts* RA RA RA!

Other verses
You put your left arm in . . .
You put your right leg in . . .
You put your left leg in . . .
You put your whole self in . . .

44

PIP, SQUEAK, AND WILFRED

At least six players are needed for this rough-and-tumble game. Choose one player to be the caller. Everyone else stands in a circle and the caller moves around naming each player as either a PIP, a SQUEAK, or a WILFRED. Once everyone knows who they are, the caller stands outside the circle and calls out a name. If she says "Squeak" then all the Squeaks must leave their places and run around the outside of the circle.

The caller can then give two different commands: "Change directions," which means start running in the opposite direction, and "Back home," which means everyone has to race around the circle back to their original places. The last one back is out and sits down.

The caller can shout out "Pip" and "Squeak" at the same time. If she calls out all three then the game can become quite a muddle!

45

1

The big ship sails on the alley, alley O.
The alley, alley O, the alley, alley O.
The big ship sails on the alley, alley O.
On the last day of September.

☆ *At least five dancers are needed but the more
the better. Start in a line, holding hands with
one dancer standing by a wall with her hand
high against the wall to make an arch (1).*

2

The captain said, "This will never never do,
Never never do, never never do."
The captain said, "This will never never do."
On the last day of September.

☆ *Sing as the dancer at the end of the line leads
everyone through the arch (2).*

The big ship sank to the bottom of the sea.
The bottom of the sea, the bottom of the sea.
The big ship sank to the bottom of the sea.
On the last day of September.

3

☆ *When the last player passes through the arch, the player making the arch will find her arm tugged under her so that she has to twist around and face the other way with her arms crossed and held up (3).*

4

☆ *The line now comes back around and through the arch made between the player nearest to the wall and her neighbor (4).*

5

We all dip our heads in the deep blue sea.
The deep blue sea, the deep blue sea.
We all dip our heads in the deep blue sea.
On the last day of September.

☆ *When the dancers have been through all the arches and all have crossed arms, they form a ring and sing the last verse — sadly (5).*

See, see, my bonny
I cannot play with you.
My sister's got the mumps,
My brother's got the flu.

Slide down the rainbow,
I'll slam the door.
See you round the back
At half past four.

HAND-CLAPPING RHYMES

Warm-ups

THE ECHO GAME

This is a good way to learn clapping rhythm. Sit in a circle with one player in the middle. This player claps out a rhythm on his shoulder, knee, or arm and everyone else must copy. Any number can play.

THE NAME GAME

Everyone sits in a circle with one player in the middle. This player claps out the rhythm for a name and if it is your rhythm you clap it back. For example:

An –war   Jes – si – ca
Clap clap   clap clap clap

Pat-a-cake, pat-a-cake, baker's man,
Bake me a cake as fast as you can;
Pat it and prick it and mark it with B,
Put it in the oven for baby and me.

☆ *A rhyme to warm up with. Clap hands*
together, then your partner's hands.

Pease porridge hot,
Pease porridge cold,
Pease porridge in the pot,
Nine days old.

Some like it hot,
Some like it cold,
Some like it in the pot,
Nine days old.

 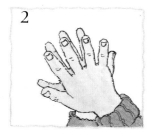  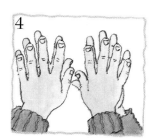

☆ *This is a basic clapping pattern. Clap hands*
together (1); your right hand with your
partner's right hand (2); your hands together
(1); your left and your partner's left (3); hands
together (1); finally both your hands and your
partner's hands clap together. Keep the sequence
going smoothly.

51

A sailor went to sea, sea, sea,
To see what he could see, see, see,
But all that he could see, see, see
Was the bottom of the deep blue
    sea, sea, sea.

☆ *On* SEA *and* SEE *clap your partner's hands three times.*

I'm Popeye the sailor man full stop.
I live in a caravan full stop.
I opened the door,
Fell flat on the floor,
I'm Popeye the sailor man full stop.
    Comma, comma, dash — dash —
    Quick flash, turn around;
    Touch the ground and start again.

☆ *At* FULL STOP, *cross hands and touch shoulders.*

☆ *For* COMMA, *close fists and put thumbs over shoulders.*

☆ *For* DASH, *smack hips.*

Three, six, nine,
The goose drank wine,
The monkey chewed tobacco
On the street car line,
The line broke,
The monkey got choked,
And they all went to heaven
In a little row boat.

☆ *Clap hands together once then right
hand to partner's right hand twice,
hands together once, then left hand
to partner's left hand twice. Repeat.*

Have you ever ever ever
In your long-legged life
Seen a long-legged sailor
With a long-legged wife?

No I've never never never
In my long-legged life
Seen a long-legged sailor
With a long-legged wife.

☆ *You can repeat this rhyme with a
knock-kneed, flat-footed, and bow-legged*
SAILOR *and* WIFE!

The rhymes

Under the bram bush,
Under the sea, boom boom boom
True love forever,
True love for me.
When we get married,
We'll have a family,
A boy for you, a girl for me,
Um tiddley um dum, cha-cha!

☆ *Try clapping vertically, right palm upward*
and left palm downward for the first beat.

My mammy told me
If I was goody
That she would buy me
A rubber dolly.
My aunty told her
I kissed a soldier
Now she won't buy me
A rubber dolly.

I'm a pretty little Dutch girl,
As pretty as can be be be.
And all the boys on the football team
Go crazy over me me me.
My boyfriend's name is Tony,
He comes from macaroni,
He's got 48 toes and a cherry on his nose
And this is how my story goes:
My boyfriend gave me an apple,
My boyfriend gave me a pear.
My boyfriend gave me 25 cents
To kiss him on the stairs stairs stairs.
I gave him back the apple,
I gave him back the pear,
I gave him back the 25 cents
And threw him down the stairs stairs stairs!

☆ *Clap three times on your knees for the repeated words. Here are more verses if you can keep the rhythm going!*

One day when I was walking
I heard my boyfriend talking
To the prettiest girl
With a strawberry curl,
And this is what she said:
I L-O-V-E love you,
I K-I double S, kiss you.
But she jumped in a lake
And swallowed a snake
And went home
With a belly ache.

Miss Mary Mack,
　　　　Mack,
　　　　Mack,
All dressed in black,
　　　　black,
　　　　black,
With silver buttons,
　　　　buttons,
　　　　buttons,
All down her back,
　　　　back,
　　　　back.
She asked her mother,
　　　　mother,
　　　　mother,
For fifteen cents,
　　　　cents,
　　　　cents,
To see the elephant,
　　　　elephant,
　　　　elephant,
Jump over the fence,
　　　　fence,
　　　　fence.
He jumped so high,
　　　　high,
　　　　high,
He reached the sky,
　　　　sky,
　　　　sky,
And never came back,
　　　　back,
　　　　back,
Till the first of July,
　　　　ly,
　　　　ly.

☆ *For each verse: Touch knees, touch shoulders, clap hands together; then clap your partner's hands three times. Spin around at the end.*

I had a little monkey,
I called him Sonny Jim,
I put him in a bathtub,
To see if he could swim;

He drank all the water,
He ate up all the soap,
He lay down on the bath mat,
Blowing bubbles from his throat.

"Mommy, Mommy, I feel ill,
Call the doctor down the hill."
In came the doctor, in came the nurse,
In came the lady with the alligator purse.

"He's naughty," said the doctor,
"He's wicked," said the nurse,
"Hiccups!" said the lady with the alligator purse.

Out went the doctor, out went the nurse,
Out went the lady with the alligator purse.

Dom dom malayas,
Sweet sweet malayas,
Sweet sweet lady,
Gimme, gimme chocomilk,
Chocomilk is out.
One, two, three.

☆ This is a very fast clapping game. Stand in a circle and choose someone to begin. He swings his right hand to clap the left hand of the player standing on his left. That player swings her right to the left and so on around the circle. The player whose hand is clapped on THREE is out of the game and the rhyme is repeated until only two players are left. These two players hold hands and rotate their wrists until OUT. Now the player whose hand is uppermost strokes the other's hand for ONE and TWO and tries to slap it on THREE. The player whose hand is being stroked can snatch his hand away to avoid the slap!

WHO STOLE THE COOKIES?

All players:	Who stole the cookie from the cookie jar?
	Number One stole the cookie from the cookie jar.
Number One:	Who, me?
All players:	Yes, you.
Number One:	Not I.
All players:	Then who?
	Who stole the cookie from the cookie jar?
Number One:	Number Eight stole the cookie from the cookie jar.
Number Eight:	Who, me?
All players:	Yes, you.
Number Eight:	Not I.
All players:	Then who?
	Who stole the cookie from the cookie jar?
Number Eight:	Number Five stole the cookie from the cookie jar.

☆ *Up to ten players can join in this game. They sit in a circle and everyone picks a number for themselves — a different number from one to ten. Everyone claps their own hands and their neighbor's alternately, and chants the words. The player who is number one picks the number of another player. This player has to quickly continue by choosing another number. He can say any number so long as it hasn't already been picked. If it has, the player calling the number is out.*

Each peach pear plum
I spy Tom Thumb.

Tom Thumb fast asleep
I spy Bo-Peep.

Bo-Peep around the corner
I spy Jack Horner.

Jack Horner up a pole
I spy King Cole.

King Cole drinking juice
I spy Mother Goose.

Mother Goose gave a shout
That means you are OUT.

DIPPING AND COUNTING-OUT RHYMES

Counting out

For many games you need to choose one player to be IT. There are lots of ways to do this.

You can call out, "Last off the ground is it" . . . or "Last to the lamppost is it."

You can make a circle with your arms and call, "Last in the bucket is it." Then the last player to put her hands into the circle is IT.

Or you can dip — use a rhyme to count people out. All the players stand in a circle or line and one player points to the others in turn saying the words. The dip can pick IT straightaway:

The one who gets to number two
Surely must be it — one TWO!

Or the rhyme can count players out and the last one left is chosen:

Red, white, and blue,
The cat's got flu,
The dog's got chicken pox,
And out goes YOU!

☆ Three ways to count out with a rhyme.

Eeny meeny miny mo
Catch a baby by the toe.
If he squeals let him go
Eeny meeny miny mo.

☆ By pointing at each player.

One potato
Two potato
Three potato
Four —
Five potato
Six potato
Seven potato
More.

☆ By counting fists.

Your shoes are dirty,
Your shoes are clean,
Your shoes are not fit
To be seen by the Queen.

☆ By counting feet.

The rhymes

Intery, mintery, cutery, corn,
Apple seed and briar thorn.
Wire, briar, limber lock,
Five geese in a flock.
One flew east and one flew west,
One flew over the cuckoo's nest.
O-U-T spells out.

Inky pinky ponky
Daddy bought a donkey.
The donkey died,
Daddy cried.
Inky pinky ponky.

Ip dip dip,
My blue ship,
Sailing on the water
Like a cup and saucer.
Ip dip dip.

Icker backer,
Soda cracker,
Icker backer boo,
Engine number nine,
Out goes you.

Ipper dipper dation,
My operation.
How many people at the station?

☆ *The last player pointed at gives a
number, for example, five.*

The one who comes to number five
Will surely not be IT.
One, two, three, four, five.

Engine, engine, number nine,
Running up Chicago line.
If the train goes off the track
Do you want your money back?
Yes, no, maybe so.

☆ *The player landed on says yes or no,
for example, yes.*

Y-E-S spells yes
So out you must go.

Ibble wobble black bobble,
Ibble wobble out,
Turn the dirty dish cloth
Inside out —
First you turn it inside,
Then you turn it out —
Ibble wobble black bobble,
Ibble wobble out.

Eenie meenie macker racker
Rari rie domi nacker
Chicker bocker lolli popper
Om pom push
Alli galli goo
Out goes you.

Eachie, peachie, pear, plum,
When does your birthday come?
One, two, three, you are out.

☆ *The last player pointed at says his*
birthday — for instance the third of
April — and the rhyme continues using
the number given.

I climbed up the apple tree,
All the apples fell on me.
Bake an apple, bake a pie,
Have you ever told a lie?

NO.

Yes you did, you know you did.
You broke your mother's teapot lid.
What color was it?

☆ *The player pointed at last chooses*
a color, for example, blue, and the rhyme continues:

No it wasn't, it was gold,
That's another lie you've told.
Out you go for saying so.

My mother bought a dress —
What color do you guess?

☆ *The player pointed at suggests a color,*
for example, red, and the rhyme continues:

R-E-D spells red.
Out you go
For saying so.

Drip drop, drip drop,
down by the sea,
Up popped a mermaid,
she said to me:
"Skip in the middle,
one at each end,
Each is a sister,
each is a friend."

SKIPPING AND BALL-BOUNCING

Warming up rhymes

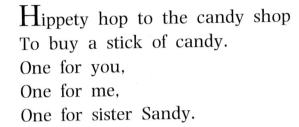

Hippety hop to the candy shop
To buy a stick of candy.
One for you,
One for me,
One for sister Sandy.

☆ *Mark two lines on the ground with skipping ropes. Hop from one to the other. Widen the gap little by little.*

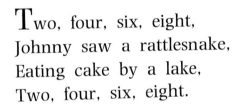

Two, four, six, eight,
Johnny saw a rattlesnake,
Eating cake by a lake,
Two, four, six, eight.

☆ *Lay the skipping rope on the ground like a snake. Try to walk along its back.*

Jack be nimble,
Jack be quick,
Jack jump over
The candlestick.

☆ *Practice jumping over objects.*

R oly poly,
Barley sugar.

☆ *Without a rope practice
skipping from one leg to the
other. Sing as you skip.*

A ndy Pandy,
Sugary Candy,
French Almond,
Nuts!

☆ *Start skipping slowly and see
how quickly you can go.*

U nder the stars
Over the moon.

☆ *The rope is held by two players — the enders
— who move it up and down chanting the
rhyme. On* UNDER *the players run under the
rope; on* OVER *they jump over it.*

Akabacka soda cracker,
Does your father chew tobacca?
Yes-No-Maybe so.
Yes-No-Maybe so . . .

☆ *Keep repeating the last line until you trip up. Whichever word you land on will give you the answer!*

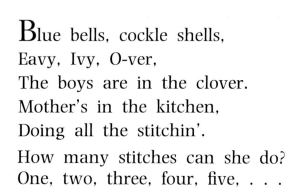

Blue bells, cockle shells,
Eavy, Ivy, O-ver,
The boys are in the clover.
Mother's in the kitchen,
Doing all the stitchin'.

How many stitches can she do?
One, two, three, four, five, . . .

☆ *When you trip up, you'll know how many stitches.*

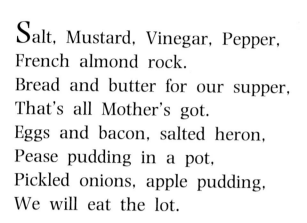

Salt, Mustard, Vinegar, Pepper,
French almond rock.
Bread and butter for our supper,
That's all Mother's got.
Eggs and bacon, salted heron,
Pease pudding in a pot,
Pickled onions, apple pudding,
We will eat the lot.

Mabel, Mabel, lay the table,
   Don't forget the
   Salt, Mustard,
   Vinegar, Pepper.

☆ *When you get to* PEPPER, *try doing
the bumps, which means turning the
rope twice in one skip.*

I like coffee,
I like tea,
I like *Jamie*,
In with me.

I hate coffee,
I hate tea,
I don't want *Jamie*,
In with me.

☆ *In this rhyme choose a friend to skip
in with you. On the second verse your
friend skips out.*

73

 Aa
1
Bb
2
Cc
3

Early in the morning at half past eight,
I heard the mailman knocking at the gate,
Up jumps *Lucy* to open the door
How many letters fell on the floor?
One, two, three, four five, . . .

Who from?
A, B, C, D, E . . .

☆ *Two people hold the rope. After* JUMPS, *they name a friend who skips until she trips. She skips until she stumbles on a number which tells her how many letters she received. Skip on to find out who sent the letters.*

Dd
4
Ee
5
Ff

I'm a girl guide, dressed in blue,
Here are the actions I must do.
Salute to the captain,
Bow to the Queen,
Turn right around
And count sixteen.
One, two, three, four,
    five, . . . sixteen.

☆ *Two people swing the rope while the skipper copies the actions of the rhyme.*

Lemon pie, apple tart.
Tell me the name of your sweetheart.
A, B, C, D, E, F . . .

Felix is your love
White doves up above,
Sitting on his knee
Under the apple tree,
Kissing one, two, three, four, . . .

☆ *Skip this game to find out who you will marry! The skipper skips until she trips. Then her friends choose someone she knows whose name begins with that letter, for example, F for Felix. Then she skips again to find out how many kisses she gets!*

Underneath the apple tree
A boy said to me —
Kiss me, cuddle me,
Who should it be?
A, B, C, D . . .
Will you get married?
Yes, no, yes, no . . .
What will he marry you in?
Silk, satin, cotton, rags . . .
How will you go to your wedding?
Coach, carriage, wheelbarrow, car . . .
How many children?
One, two, three, four, five, . . .

☆ *Two people hold the rope and everyone takes it in turns to find out their future. The players recite the alphabet, repeat* YES *and* NO *and so on after each question. The letter or word the skipper trips on gives the answer to the question.*

6

Gg

7

Hh

8

Ii

9

Jj

10

☆ Two players hold the rope and everyone takes it in turns to skip.

Bumper car, bumper car,
Number forty-eight,
Whizzed round the cooooorner

☆ The skipper leaves the rope, runs right around one end and runs in again.

And slammed on the brakes.

☆ The skipper traps the rope between his legs and starts skipping again.

Brakes didn't work,
Slid down the hill,
Landed in the duck pond
And then stood still.
How many fish can you see?
one, two, three, four, five, . . .

☆ The one with the highest number of fish before he trips wins the game.

Teddy bear, teddy bear
  Turn around.
Teddy bear, teddy bear,
  Touch the ground.

Teddy bear, teddy bear,
  Hands on head.
Teddy bear, teddy bear,
  Go to bed.

Teddy bear, teddy bear,
  Jump the stairs.
Teddy bear, teddy bear,
  Say your prayers.

Teddy bear, teddy bear,
  Turn out the light.
Teddy bear, teddy bear,
  Spell goodnight.

☆ Two players swing the rope and everyone takes it in turn to skip in and do the actions, spelling out GOODNIGHT *at the end.*

G-O-O-D  N-I-G-H-T

Not last night
But the night before
Twenty-four robbers
Came knocking at my door.
Went downstairs to let them in
And this is what I saw:

Spanish lady, Spanish lady,
Do high kicks.

Spanish lady, Spanish lady,
Take a bow.

Spanish lady, Spanish lady,
That's all for now.

☆ *Two players swing the rope. Everyone takes it in turns to skip in, in pairs, and do the actions.*

I went to the animal fair,
The birds and the beasts were there.
By the light of the moon the gay baboon
Was combing his golden hair.
The monkey fell out of his bunk
Slid down the elephant's trunk.
The elephant sneezed
And fell on his knees
And what became of the monkey,
Monkey, monkey,
Monkey, monk!

☆ *Two players swing the rope. Everyone skips in.*
If someone makes a mistake, he is out. Skip on
until only one person is left in.

All in together,
No matter what the weather.
I spy Jack,
Peeping through a crack.
One, two, three,
Busy, busy, bee,
Nineteen, twenty,
Leave the rope empty.

January, February, March, April,
May, June, July, August,
September, October,
November, December.

☆ *Two players hold the rope. Everyone else*
skips, jumping out on their birth month.

79

Ball-bouncing

Solid rubber balls are best for bouncing games.

Bounce the ball on the ground and pat it down again.

Or bounce the ball against a wall and catch it.

Try putting the ball inside the toe of an old stocking. Bounce the ball from side to side against a wall.

Chant a rhyme as you bounce or
catch the ball.

Bouncie bouncie ballie,
My friend Paulie,
I gave her a slap,
She gave me one back,
Bouncie, bouncie ballie.

Mickey Mouse came to my house
I asked him what he'd like —
A sunset smile,
A crocodile,
A ride upon my bike.

One, two, three,
Mother caught a flea,
She salted it and peppered it
And served it up for tea!

81

Types of bounces

Here are ten ways to bounce a ball against a wall.

Overs
Throwing the ball overarm or straight at a wall.

Unders
Throwing the ball underarm or under your leg.

Dropsies
Throw the ball against a wall and let it bounce on the ground before catching it.

Bouncies
Bounce the ball on the ground once and catch it as it comes off the wall.

Backsies
Throw the ball against a wall from behind your back, turn around, catch.

Onesies
Catch the ball with one hand.

Twosies
Catch the ball with two hands.

Turnsies
Throw the ball against a wall, spin right around, and catch.

Clapsies
Throw the ball and clap once before catching.

Stampsies
Throw the ball and stamp your feet once before catching.

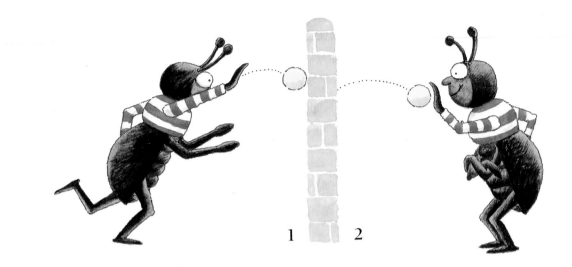

1   2

Big black bug
Sitting on a rug —
I one it,
I two it,
I three it,
I four it,
I five it,
I six it,
I seven it.
You ate it!

3

4

☆ *In this game, you have to try seven different kinds of bounces — without dropping the ball.*

5   6   7

Oliver-Oliver-Oliver Twist
Bet you a dollar you can't do this:
Number one — touch your tongue,
Number two — touch your shoe,
Number three — touch your knee,
Number four — touch the floor,
Number five — be alive,
Number six — pick up sticks,
Number seven — jump to Heaven,
Number eight — shut the gate,
Number nine — walk the line,
Number ten — start again.

☆ *As you bounce the ball, carry out each action.*

A mimsy, a clapsy
   Roll my hands, touch backsie
My right hand, my left hand
   High as the sky, low as the sea
I touch my knee and my heel and
   my toe
   And over we go.

☆ *Follow the actions. Pass your leg over the ball on* OVER WE GO.

Charlie Chaplin went to France
To teach the ladies how to dance.
This is what he taught them:
   Heel, toe, and over you go!
   Heel, toe, and over you go!
   Heel, toe, and over you go!

☆ *On the first three lines just bounce the ball. On* HEEL *tap the ground with your heel. On* TOE *tap the ground with your toe. On* OVER YOU GO *pass your leg over the ball.*

PIGGY–IN–THE–MIDDLE

You need three people but you can play with more. Dip (see page 62) to decide who will be PIGGY and stand in the middle. Piggy then has to try to catch the ball as the others throw it backward and forward.

SCORE THROW

Any number can play this ball game. With chalk, draw some shapes on a wall and write a number — the score — inside each one. Give the smaller shapes a higher score. Everyone stands back from the wall behind a line drawn on the ground. No one is allowed over the line. Everyone has three turns to throw the ball against the wall and score as much as they can.

HOOP CATCH

You need four players for this game. Two stand in the middle and hold a hoop between them. The others stand on either side and throw the ball backward and forward through the hoop. If someone drops it, she has to take a turn holding the hoop.

DEAD DONKEYS

Any number can play. Everyone stands in a circle and throws the ball around. If anyone drops the ball, he says the letter D. If the same person misses again, he says the letter O. If he misses a third time, he says the letter N, then K, E, and Y. When he has spelled out D-O-N-K-E-Y, he is out. The last one left wins. The others are DEAD DONKEYS.

SPUD

This game is played with as many people as possible. It requires a *soft* sponge ball.

One person is chosen to start and she throws the ball into the air and calls out the name of another player. That player runs to catch or fetch the ball while everyone else scatters. When the player gets the ball, he throws it at another player. If he misses, then he loses one SPUD. If he hits someone with the ball, then that player has to try to hit someone else. If the player misses three times and loses three SPUDS, then he has to bend over and let all the others throw the ball at him — from a distance!

QUEENIE

This guessing game is for five or more players. Start by dipping (see page 62) to choose who will be QUEENIE. She turns her back on the other players and throws the ball over her shoulder. The player nearest the ball picks it up and hides it behind his back. When Queenie turns around everyone sings:

Queenie, Queenie, who's got the ball?
Is she big or is she small?
Is she fat or is she thin?
Or is she like a rolling pin?

Queenie then runs around the players looking for the ball. But they spin around so she can't see who has it. Queenie then guesses who has the ball by pointing at someone, and he has to show his hands one by one and say, "I haven't got it." If she guesses right the first time, she carries on as Queenie. If she doesn't, then the player with the ball becomes Queenie.

Girls and boys come out to play,
The moon doth shine as bright as day.
Leave your supper and leave your sleep,
Come join your playfellows in the street.
Come with a whoop and come with a call,
Come with a good will or not at all.
Up the ladder and down the wall,
A half-penny loaf will serve us all;
You find milk, and I'll find flour,
And we'll have a pudding in half an hour.

HIDING, GUESSING, TICKLING, AND CHASING

Hiding
and guessing

Peek-a-boo, peek-a-boo,
Who's that hiding there?
Peek-a-boo, peek-a-boo,
   Tom's behind the chair.

☆ *Change the name* TOM *to that of the person you are playing with.*

Handy dandy,
Riddledy ro.
Which hand will you have,
High or low?

☆ *Start by hiding a small object in one clenched fist. The other player has to guess which hand it is in. If she guesses correctly, it is her turn to hide the object; otherwise she must guess again.*

Hurly burly trump a tray
   The goat was bought on market day.
Peter Piper hunt a buck.
   How many horns now stand up?

☆ *One player covers her eyes while the other holds up a number of fingers and chants the rhyme. The game is to guess the number of fingers held up.*

COBBLER, COBBLER

Cobbler, Cobbler, mend my shoe.
Get it done by half past two.
Stitch it up and stitch it down.
Then I'll give you half a crown.

Choose one person to be IT. Everyone else sits cross-legged in a circle. IT walks around holding a shoe (or other object) while the rhyme is chanted. Then she tosses the shoe into the circle and turns her back. The others hide the shoe, then IT has to find it. She runs around the circle and the players can pass the shoe under their crossed legs to make things more difficult. Whoever has the shoe when IT manages to get it starts the game again. At least six players are needed.

GOOD MORNING, YOUR MAJESTY

This game is for at least five players. One player is chosen to be the QUEEN and sits on a "throne." She has her eyes blindfolded so she cannot see. One by one everyone creeps up and whispers into her ear, "Good morning, Your Majesty!"

Everyone disguises their voice to make it difficult to guess who they are. If the Queen guesses correctly, then that player sits down. If she cannot guess — or gets it wrong — then it is that player's turn to be King or Queen.

BLIND MAN'S BLUFF

Blind man, blind man,
    Sure you can't see?
Turn around three times,
    And try and catch me.
Turn east, turn west.
    Catch as you can,
Did you think you caught me?
    Blind, blind man!

☆ *One player is blindfolded and then has to catch another player and guess who it is.*

I DRAW A SNAKE

You need at least four players for this game. Start by choosing one player to be IT. IT turns his back and hides his face in his hands. Everyone else gathers around and one player draws a snake on his back chanting:

I draw a snake upon your back,
Who will put in the eye?

Someone else then pokes in the eye. IT now turns around and has to guess who put in the eye. But before he does, he sets a task — for instance, he might say, "The person who put in the eye must do a handstand;" ["Run down to the end of the street;" or "Jump up and down fifty times."] Then he makes his guess. If he guesses correctly, then that player must carry out the task. If he is wrong, then he has to do the task himself!

As he tries to guess, the others can chant:

I spread butter,
I spread cheese,
I spread jam
Upon your knees.
Guess who tipped you.

HIDE AND SEEK

Play this game with as many people as possible. The player who is IT closes her eyes and counts up to twenty or more while everyone else scatters and hides. When she reaches twenty, she shouts, "Coming — ready or not." The last player to be found is the winner.

BUG IN THE RUG

In this game if you are found you can run for "home." If you get there without being touched, then you are safe.

TOAD IN THE HOLE

In this game if you are found then you join in looking for the others.

CUCKOO

In this game only one player hides and everyone else seeks.

CRANEY CROW

Chickamy, chickamy, craney crow,
I went to the well to wash my toe.
When I got back, my chickens were gone.
What time is it, Old Witch?
One o'clock, two o'clock, three . . .

☆ *The seeker is the* WITCH *and the others are the* CHICKENS *and they hide while the rhyme is chanted and the hours one to twelve are counted. Then the witch looks for the chickens.*

97

SARDINES

Any number of people can play this game, and it is best played indoors where there are lots of good places to hide. One player is chosen to be the SARDINE and he goes off to hide. After a while everyone splits up to look for him. If a player finds the sardine, then she hides with him. It can get quite a squash!

The last player to find the sardine is the loser and has to begin the next game. Sometimes Sardines is called Squashed Tomatoes.

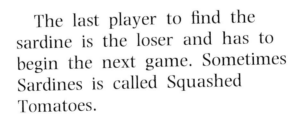

KICK THE CAN

Play this game with as many people as possible. If you don't have a tin can, a lump of wood or a stone will do. The tin can is placed on the ground as the home base. Using a dip, choose a player to be IT.

IT kicks the can hard, and while he is putting it back on home base, everyone else scatters and hides.

IT then searches, and if he sees anyone hiding, he can capture her by putting his foot on the can and calling her name.

123
I see
Lisa

The players who are captured have to stand by home base and can only be released by a free player running up and kicking the can away.

Riddle-me-ree

☆ *Try and guess these riddles.*

Little Nancy Etticoat,
With a white petticoat,
And a red nose;
She has no feet or hands,
The longer she stands,
The shorter she grows.

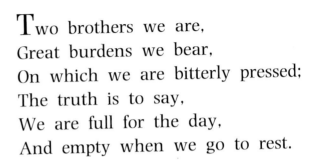

Two brothers we are,
Great burdens we bear,
On which we are bitterly pressed;
The truth is to say,
We are full for the day,
And empty when we go to rest.

I have a little sister, they call her peep peep,
She wades the waters deep, deep, deep;
She climbs the mountains high, high, high;
Poor little creature she has but one eye.

Thirty white horses
Upon a red hill,
Now they stamp,
Now they champ,
Now they stand still.

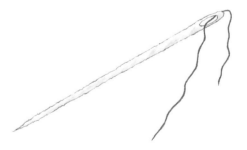

A house full, a hole full,
You cannot gather a bowl full.

Old Mother Twitchett has but one eye,
And a long tail which she can let fly,
And every time she goes over a gap,
She leaves a bit of her tail in a trap.

In marble halls as white as milk,
Lined with a skin as soft as silk,
Within a fountain crystal clear,
A golden apple doth appear.
No doors there are to this stronghold,
Yet thieves break in and steal the gold.

In spring I am dressed,
Decked out in my best,
In summer more clothing I wear;
When colder it grows,
I fling off my clothes,
And in winter quite naked appear.

Purple, yellow, red, and green,
The King cannot reach it, nor yet the Queen,
Nor can Old Noll, whose power's so great;
Tell me this riddle while I count eight.

Flour of England, fruit of Spain,
Met together in a shower of rain;
Put in a bag, tied round with a string;
If you tell me this riddle,
I'll give you a ring.

I'm called by the name of a man,
Yet am as little as a mouse;
When winter comes I love to be
With my red target near the house.

Ticklers

Can you keep a secret?
I don't suppose you can.
You musn't laugh or smile
While I tickle your hand.

Davy, Davy, Dumpling
Boil him in the pot.
Sugar him and butter him,
Eat him while he's hot.

☆ *Change the name* DAVY *to that of the person you are tickling.*

☆ *An unusual traditional toe counting — and tickling — rhyme.*

This little pig had a rub-a-dub,
This little pig had a scrub-a-scrub,

Criss, cross
Applesauce,
Spiders climbing up your back.
Cool breeze,
Tight squeeze,
And now you've got the shivers.

☆ *Sketch a cross for* CROSS;
tickle back for SPIDERS; *blow*
for the BREEZE; *hug for*
SQUEEZE; *and shake gently on*
SHIVERS.

This little pig-a-wig ran upstairs,
This little pig-a-wig called out, "Bears!"

Down came the jar with a loud slim slam!
And this little pig had all the jam.

Games of Chase...Catch...Tip...Tiggy.

The simplest way to play touch chase is for the person who is IT to touch another player and then he or she becomes IT. Choose who will be IT by using a dip (see page 62).

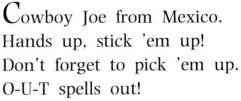

Cowboy Joe from Mexico.
Hands up, stick 'em up!
Don't forget to pick 'em up.
O-U-T spells out!

In these games, the rules are all different.

1

Tunnel Touch
When you are caught, put one arm against something to make a tunnel. If someone else runs under your arm, you are free.

2

Ticky Leapfrog
If you are touched, you crouch down. When someone leapfrogs over you, you are free.

3

Off-ground Tiggy
You are safe from being touched by finding a place that is off the ground — but you are not allowed to stay there too long!

4

Colors
Everyone decides on a color. If you are touching that color then you are safe.

5

Shadow Tick
This time you catch someone by touching her shadow with your foot. It doesn't count if you touch *her* at all!

6

Three-Squat Tag
If you are about to be caught, you can bob down and touch the ground. Then you are safe. But you can only do this three times in a game!

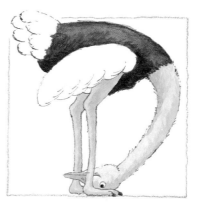

7

Stick-in-the-Mud
If you are touched you are frozen to the spot like a statue. When another player touches your hand, you are free.

8

Touch Wood or Iron
If you are touching wood or iron, then you are safe.

9

Underground He
If you are caught, stand with your legs open wide. If someone crawls under your legs, you are free.

POISON

This game is for three or more players. One player is chosen to be IT and she holds out her hands. Everyone else holds on to one of her fingers. IT says, "I went to the moon and bought some . . ." and she lists foods beginning with the letter **p**, such as peas or pancakes. But if she says POISON, everyone has to run for it. She chases after them and the first player who is caught becomes IT. If a player lets go and starts running before IT says POISON, then he is out before the game has even started!

SHOPPING

At least four people are required for this game. One player is chosen to be MOTHER and she tells her CHILDREN (everyone else) that she is going shopping. She gives each of them a job to do while she is away, for example, sweeping, cleaning, straightening up, mowing the lawn, or digging the garden. Then she pretends to go shopping and all the children creep up to listen to what she is going to buy. Mother says out loud all the things she is buying. For example: "I'd like to buy a . . . new coffeepot, a plate, some bananas . . ." She buys a number of different things until suddenly she says, "I'd like to buy a . . . cane to beat my children with!" Then everyone runs for it! The first player who is caught is the next mother.

WHAT'S THE TIME, MR. WOLF?

You need at least five people — the more that play the better. One player is chosen to be MR. WOLF.

Mr. Wolf walks around and everyone else follows — at a safe distance — calling, "What's the time, Mr. Wolf?" Mr. Wolf replies, "One o'clock" or "Two o'clock" and so on until suddenly he shouts, "Dinnertime — and I'm coming to get you!"

And with that he chases after everyone. You can only escape if you make it to your home base. But the first player who is caught becomes the next Mr. Wolf.

PUSS IN THE CORNER

You need five players. One player is chosen to be the CAT. The other four players (the RATS) stand around four points as if they were on a large square. The cat stalks around looking for a free corner. When the others think it is safe, they run from corner to corner. The cat tries to reach an empty place first. The players on each corner make the cat very angry by calling out, "Puss, puss, come for your milk!"

In the land of Mars
The cats smoke cigars,
The rats play football
And the mice drive cars.

DRAGON TAG

For this game at least ten players are needed.
Four players join arms to make the DRAGON.
The dragon has to try to catch everyone else. It
can only do this by making a circle around a
player. As soon as a player is caught, he must
link onto the back of the dragon. The game is
over when everyone has been circled and is part
of one long dragon.

I'm the Monster of Loch Ness
And my name you'll never guess.
I can dance in a ring,
I can do the Highland Fling,
For I'm the Monster of Loch Ness.

GLUEPOTS

A game for as many people as possible. One player is chosen to be IT and has to chase the others. Before the game starts, IT picks a number of special places to put the people she catches. These are her GLUEPOTS and anyone who is put there cannot move. They can be released only if a free player touches their hand — but if the free player makes a mistake and puts a foot into the gluepot, then he is stuck there too!

RED LION

You need at least four players. One player is chosen to be IT — the LION. The lion has a den. Everyone else has a home base as far away as possible from the lion's den. The players chant:

Red Lion, Red Lion,
Come out of your den.
Whoever you catch
Can be one of your men.

The lion chases everyone and they all have to run for home base to be safe. If the lion touches anyone three times before she gets home, he can take her back to his den. She then becomes a lion too.

How many miles to Babylon?
Three score miles and ten.
Can I get there by candlelight?
Yes, and back again.
If your heels are nimble and light,
You may get there by candlelight.

BABYLON

This game is for at least seven players. Choose one person to be the catcher. Everyone else splits into two teams and stands in two lines on either side.

One side chants:
"How many miles to Babylon?"
The others reply:
"Three score miles and ten."
The first side asks:
"Can we get there by candlelight?"
The others reply:
"Yes, if your legs are long and light,
There and back again."

Then both sides rush across trying not to be caught by the catcher in the middle. The ones who are caught stand in the middle and become catchers too. Four hundred years ago this game was known as "Barley-Break."

FOX IN THE WALL

This game is for six or more players. One player is chosen to be the FARMER, one player is the FOX, and all the others are GEESE. The farmer leaves the geese and goes far away. The fox finds a place to hide between the farmer and the geese. This is his den.

The farmer calls: "Geese, geese, come home."

Geese: "We are frightened."
Farmer: "What of?"

Geese: "The fox."
Farmer: "The fox has gone away and won't be back today. Geese, geese, come home."

The geese then run toward the farmer, and the fox tries to catch one and take it back to his den.

112

FARMER, FARMER

At least four players are required
but the more that play the better.
One player is chosen to be the
FARMER. Everyone else lines up in
front of her and calls out: "Farmer,
farmer, may we cross your golden river?"

The farmer replies, picking a color:
"Only if you have *red*."

Anyone wearing this color can
cross safely. The others have to
dash across the river. If the farmer
catches them, then they are out.

☆ *Some alternative ways to
ask to cross the river.*

Old Mother Witch,
may we cross
your ditch?

Farmer, farmer,
may we pass
over the hills
and over the
grass?

Please Mr. Crocodile,
may we cross the
water in a cup and
saucer upside down?

Please Mr. Porter,
may we cross your
golden water to see
your fairy daughter
drink a cup of water?

CROWS AND CRANES

This game is for two teams with at least five players on each team. There is also a caller. One player is chosen to be the caller and stands in the middle. Everyone else splits up into the teams called CROWS and CRANES. The Crows stand at one end of the room or garden and the Cranes stand at the opposite end.

When they are ready, the caller shouts, "Start walking!"

Both teams march toward the middle. As they get closer, the caller calls out the name of one of the teams — Crows or Cranes. Whichever team he names has to chase the others and try to touch them before they get back to their home base. The players who are caught have to join the other side and the team with the largest number wins. The caller can make things more interesting by keeping each side waiting to know which team will be called: "Crrrrr...anes!"

You can also play Rats and Rabbits, Black and Blue, Crusts and Crumbs.

☆ *An old-fashioned dancing game for eight or more players. Divide into two equal teams and stand apart facing each other.*

Here we go gathering nuts in May,
Nuts in May, nuts in May,
Here we go gathering nuts in May,
On a cold and frosty morning.

☆ *Both sides advance and retreat singing.*

Who will you have for nuts in May,
Nuts in May, nuts in May,
Who will you have for nuts in May,
On a cold and frosty morning?

☆ *One side advances and retreats singing.*

Who will you have to pull her away,
Pull her away, pull her away,
Who will you have to pull her away,
On a cold and frosty morning?

☆ *The first side advances and retreats singing.*

We'll have *Carla* for nuts in May,
Nuts in May, nuts in May,
We'll have *Carla* for nuts in May,
On a cold and frosty morning.

☆ *The other side advances and retreats naming someone from the other team.*

We'll have *John* to pull her away,
Pull her away, pull her away,
We'll have *John* to pull her away,
On a cold and frosty morning.

☆ *The other side names one of their own team.*

☆ *Then the two players meet in the middle for a tug-of-war. Whoever loses joins the winner's side. The game is repeated until one side has all the players. The only other rule is that no one is allowed to do the pulling away twice.*

Fairy Step
A tiny step,
heel to toe.

Giant Steps
Steps as large
as possible.

Banana Slide
Slip forward on one
foot and stand
where you reach.

MAY I?

Four players are required but the game is better if there are more. One player is chosen to be IT. Everyone else stands in a line. IT shouts out someone's name and tells them what action they must do and how many times they should do it. So, she may call out a player and say, "*Kelly* may take two fairy steps." Kelly must then answer, "May I?" and take two tiny steps forward. The caller gives everyone a chance to move forward but if anyone forgets to say "May I?" they have to go back to the start. The winner is the player who reaches the caller first.

Thomas may take a banana slide

Scissors
Jump forward with
your legs apart.

LETTERS

At least three players are needed but any number can play. One player is chosen to be IT. Everyone else stands in a line. IT calls out a letter, and if it is in a player's name, that player can take a step forward. The first player to reach IT is the winner.

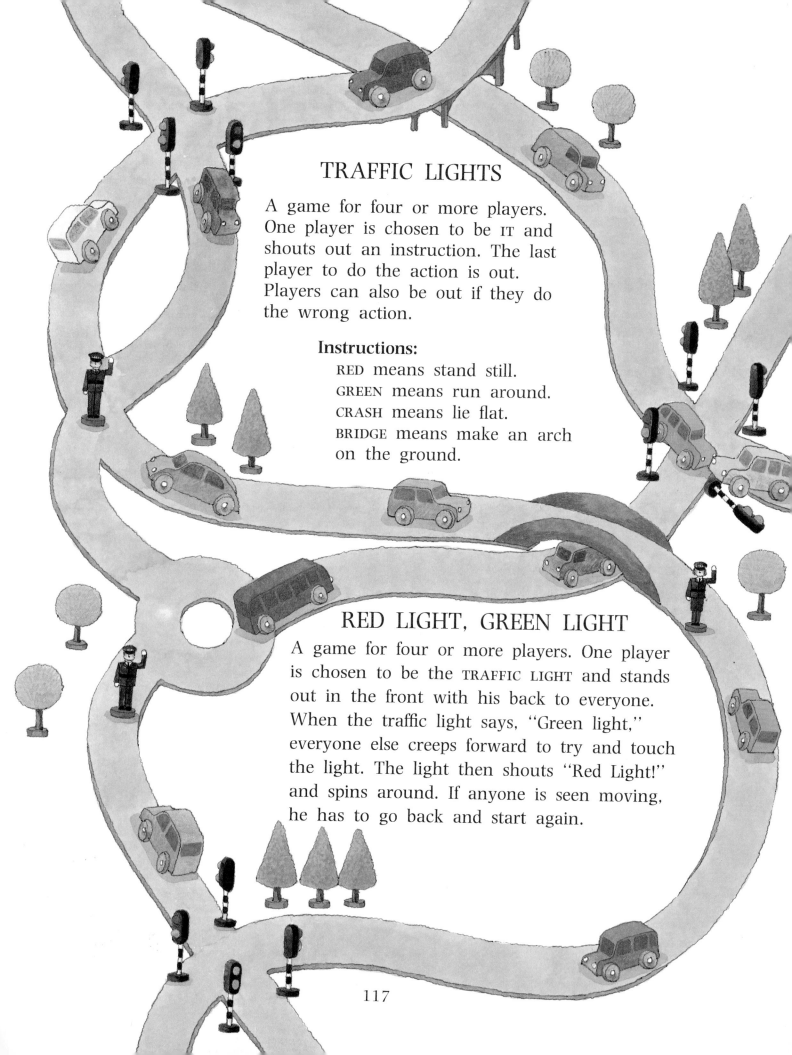

TRAFFIC LIGHTS

A game for four or more players. One player is chosen to be IT and shouts out an instruction. The last player to do the action is out. Players can also be out if they do the wrong action.

Instructions:

RED means stand still.
GREEN means run around.
CRASH means lie flat.
BRIDGE means make an arch on the ground.

RED LIGHT, GREEN LIGHT

A game for four or more players. One player is chosen to be the TRAFFIC LIGHT and stands out in the front with his back to everyone. When the traffic light says, "Green light," everyone else creeps forward to try and touch the light. The light then shouts "Red Light!" and spins around. If anyone is seen moving, he has to go back and start again.

INDEX OF RHYMES AND GAMES

SUBJECT INDEX

Games for small groups

Games for large groups

Party games

Boisterous games